DEVOTIONAL NUGGETS

30 Day Journal

Author and Writer

Rosie M. Bailes

To order additional copies of this book, contact:
Xlibris
844-714-8691
www.Xlibris.com
Orders@Xlibris.com

ISBN: Softcover   979-8-3694-2635-7 (sc)
          EBook   979-8-3694-2634-0 (e)

Print information available on the last page

Rev. date: 08/13/2024

Contents

Endorsement

A few years ago many were wearing brightly colored silicone bracelets with the acronym W.W.J.D. The acronym W.W.J.D. means "What Would Jesus Do?" As individuals face different situations the bracelet would remind them to recall what Jesus would do in a given situation. In the Devotional Nuggets 30-Day Journal, Rosie gives us an example of what Jesus would do as He attempted to convey the love and favor of God to others.

Jesus used parables to convey His message, giving clarity and encouragement to His hearers. The word parable is derived from the word "paraballo." The prefix "para" means "alongside" and "ballo" means to throw. A parable is throwing a (spiritual) truth alongside something familiar to aid in understanding something complex. A parable starts out as a picture of something familiar and common, then moves to illustrate and make plain a deeper truth.

When Jesus said "I am the vine, and you are the branches" they could identify with this picture. They were very familiar with vineyards in that region and knew that branches depended on the vine to live. It was a window so that our listeners see God and His truth and ultimately receive it.

In the Devotional Nuggets 30-Day Journal, Rosie communicates just as Jesus did, taking familiar things and experiences and allowing us to see the beautiful ways they can have spiritual meaning.

Through the nuggets in her devotional, she has the uncanny ability to take that which is commonplace and allow us to see the hand and mind of God, even in what may seem mundane and ordinary.

We all know that gold nuggets have to be dug from the dirt, polished, and presented in a way to be received by the masses. The "Nuggets" that Rosie presents in the Devotional Nuggets 30-Day Journal are nuggets that she has dug up, polished, and presented to us, for our encouragement, to help us draw closer to God, and to help us love one another, and to see God in everything.

Nuggets, by definition, are small but very valuable. Rosie's "nuggets" are compact and concise daily deposits, but very valuable nuggets that will make a tremendous impact as you walk this journey called life. All of us need encouragement, all of us need a "pickup" from time to time, and the Devotional Nuggets 30-Day Journal is that resource for us.

I encourage you to take your time and enjoy every nugget that is presented as it will give you the strength, wisdom, and guidance to be all that God has ordained for you to be. A blessing awaits you in the pages of the Devotional Nuggets 30-Day Journal.

Rev. Brian D. Hunter, M.A.
Senior Pastor
Berkeley Mt. Zion Baptist Church

Endorsement

Ms Rosi, my friend of over 35 years,

HOW REFRESHING!!

Amid the chaos, confusion, controversy, conflict and challenges in our world and lives, there is a dire need for a solution. Such has been provided through your inspired written word.

We have been ENLIGHTENED with knowledge.
We have been ENCOURAGED with hope and support.
We have been EQUIPPED with advice and necessary tools.
We have been EMPOWERED with strength and confidence.
Therefore, we can now walk with the assurance of an enriched life in Christ.

Respectfully,
Ladi Ana Jo Thompson
Former First Lady, Berkeley Mt. Zion M.B.C.
Berkeley, CA

Endorsement

I met the author Rosie at an early age, at Mt. Zion M.B.C., Oakland, CA where we grew up together. Rosie is a dedicated and committed individual. She was the one who accepted a project or assignment and wouldn't stop until it was completed. Just like this project, she isn't a quitter.

These nuggets will lead you on a path to great joy and many blessings. Yes, she still Hold on to these teachings in her daily walk of life. Thank you for not wavering from your teachings and your faith. Most of all thank you for sharing and caring.

Your Brother in Christ,

Eddie A.

Endorsement

Gran-Friend Sis. Rosie Bailes book, Devotional Nuggets, is destined to go down in history as one of the simplest tools the Holy Spirit will use to transform the lives of those already in HIS KINGDOM and those who are headed toward HIS KINGDOM. Nuggets are defined as anything of value or significance. Devotional Nuggets are valuable and significant for every child of God to be able to use healthy life giving approaches to help each of us to understand and to maneuver the challenges we face in today's world. I love the way the book is structured, and how every NUGGET is simple to read. In this book, Sis. Bailes teaches in such a way that a child is able to tune into the heart of God and take these everyday practical applications to develop confidence in God and to trust God to help them navigate the many waves one may experience in life. Devotional Nuggets is a true testament to what God has for you; will reach you and there's nothing anybody can do about it. For HIS Glory.

Love Always,
Servant L

Endorsement

All scripture is inspired by God and profitable for teaching, for reproof, for correction, for training in righteousness; so that the man of God may be adequate, equipped for every good work. @ Tim. 3:16, 17.

A nugget is a small lump of something, especially gold. ...pure high-grade gold nuggets. A nugget of information is an interesting or useful piece of information. (Collins English Dictionary)

What I can tell you about this Devotional Nuggets - 30 Day Journal is, God has poured into and downloaded into Rosie a fresh wind of down to earth, put it where the goats can get it - precious nuggets for everyday, practical, enlightening and inspiring lessons that leads you to look at yourself and your life a little differently. Rosie is always pointing us towards the Savior and laying out lessons to teach us, rebuke us, correct us, train us so that we are adequate and equipped for every good work.

Rosie is my God-mother and I have known her most of my life. These lessons, the way they are written and illustrated and the songs that go along with them are so wonderful. I can hear Rosie telling these stories and singing these songs which are so dear to her and me. What a treasure chest of goodness. You will not be disappointed when you delve into these devotional nuggets - 30 day Journal. Enjoy and get ready to draw closer to the Savior.

All for His Glory - in His Grip Always

Shirley

How This Book Came to Be

(The Birth)

To My Readers,

With the guidance of the Holy Spirit, many prayers and thought has gone into the Preparation and the completion of this book.

On Saturday, November 6, 2021, I accepted the assignment of devotional leader of the Deaconess Ministry at Berkeley Mount Zion Baptist Church, Berkeley California. Reverend Brian D. Hunter, Pastor.

After accepting the assignment, I thought about wanting the opening of our meeting to be different than the usual opening. I ask the Lord, how could the opening be different? He gave me the idea to present "DEVOTIONAL NUGGETS."

As you read these nuggets you will see that I selected different subjects, talk about them from a natural and spiritual point of view with scripture references then ending with a word of encouragement and a suggested song or songs.

About four months into my writing, my brother Eddie Bailes (AKA) Pete, asked me, Rosie, have you ever given any thought to putting your writing into book form? My answer was NO. Some hours later on the same day I was talking to my friend Dorothy Strickland and I read one of my writings to her. When I finished reading she asked me, Rosie, have you ever thought about putting your writings into book form? I was Surprised that I was asked the same question again in less than eight hours. Again, my answer was No. After pondering and praying about the question, I took this as confirmation to go forth with the project.

Of course doubt raised its head up. I questioned myself, Rosie? write a book? The Lord helped me to defeat doubt, because He brought to my memory, Philippians 4:13, which says: I CAN DO ALL THINGS THROUGH CHRIST WHICH STRENGTHENS ME. After reciting this scripture, I asked myself, Why shouldn't I go forth? After all, I already had a jump start.

As you read these pages it is my prayer that you will be informed, uplifted, encouraged, guided, inspired, and enlightened. Most of all, if you don't know Christ as your Savior and Lord, I pray that something on these pages will help you to know how you can be led to know the Savior.

Because He Lives, We too Shall Live.

Rosie M. Bailes

Dedications

This book is dedicated to my fourth brother Eddie Bailes. He is affectionately known as uncle Pete, Eddie and or Edward to others. Pete passed away on May 17, 2023. I also would like to dedicate this book to one of my number one supporters, Leroy Bailes, my brother, who recently passed on July 8, 2024. Thank you both for encouraging me to compile my Devotional Nuggets to be put into book form.

Acknowledgements

First, I thank the Holy Spirit for leading and guiding me throughout my writings. For those who allowed me to read to you, thank you. You listened, made suggestions and corrections without altering my original thoughts. To Mama, and Dottye even though you're not here with me now, thank you for seeing that I got the foundation that I am now standing on. To those who prayed for, with and encouraged me, thank you. Whatever part you had in making this devotional come into existence, a heartfelt thanks to you as well.

Acronyms

Upward
Pressing
Living
Intentionally
For
The
Eternal
Destination

God
Ultimately
Insists
Dependence
Every
Day

I
Need
Sincere
Prayers
In
Reality
Everyday
Diligently

Everyone
Needs
Christ
Our
Unmatched
Ruler
Always
Giving
Excellence
Divinely

Embrace
New
Life
In
God's
Holy
Temple
Every
Nation
Exalt Him
Diligently

Imparting
News
For
Our
Redeemer
Most
Excitingly
Delivered

Unity and Love

Unity does not just happen, we have to work at it. So many times differences among people can lead to division. This shouldn't be in the church. Instead of us concentrating on what divides us, wouldn't it be nice to concentrate on what unites us. That is ONE BODY, ONE SPIRIT, ONE LORD, ONE FAITH, ONE BAPTISM. Ephesians 4:1-6 KJV.

Have you learned to appreciate people who are different from you? Different gifts, ideas, talents and viewpoints can help the church grow as it does God's work. Let us learn to appreciate and uplift each other the way we as members of the body of Christ compliment each other.

One anothering one another is Unity and showing God's Love.

Suggested Song
   We Are One In The Spirit

Reflections:

Jesus The Light of The World

! John 1:5 states; Then this is the message which we have heard of him and declare unto you. That God is light and in Him there is no darkness at all !!!!! Jesus is the light of the world, the generator of light and we are the circuits.

As believers we should strive daily to apply Matthew 5:15-16 KJV to our life. Neither do men light a candle and put it under a bushel, but on a candlestick and it giveth light unto all that are in the house, Verse 16: Let your light so shine before men that they may see your good works and glorify your father which is in heaven.

What is this saying to us??? It is instructing us to do good works, Don't Hide our light. Let it stand out, let it glow, let it illuminate, shine for Jesus so that others will see His light in us!!!!

To be equipped and able to do this, we MUST stay plugged in and connected to the generator Jesus, who is the main source of POWER and LIGHT.

Walking on this journey we walk in different shoes as we walk in the SAME light.!!! I leave you with these (3) questions:

1. Are you plugged in and connected to the generator of light?
2. Are you walking in the light?
3. Is your light shining?

Readers, I encourage you to stay connected to the light of the world, Jesus!!! If you are not connected, I recommend that you get connected. Here's how. It's as simple as ABC. **A**-ADMIT THAT YOU ARE A SINNER, **B**-BELIEVE IN HIS DEATH BURIAL AND RESURRECTION. AND **C**ONFESS THAT YOU BELIEVE.

... FOLLOW THE ABC'S and you will be saved and connected.

Suggested Songs
Walk In The Light
This Little Light
Shine On Me

Reflections:

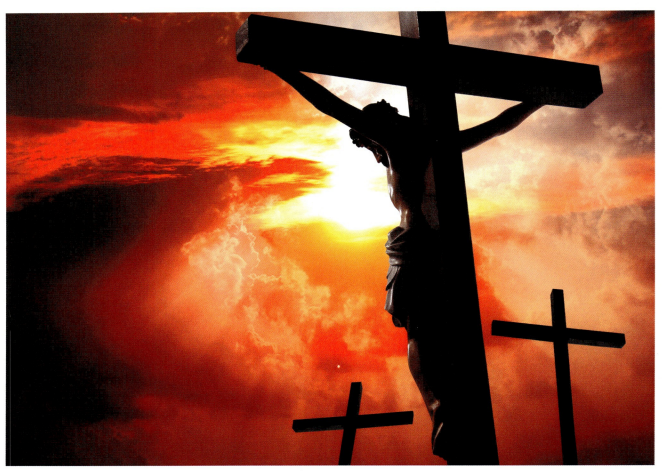

Jesus died to set you and me free
That's love.

Love

Webster states that cupid is the god of love. However we know that God, spelled with a capital G, is love. First John 4:8 KJV says, He that loveth not knoweth not God; for God is love.

There are three(3) types of love: 1. Eros- romantic, 2. Phillo-friendship/ affectionate, 3. Agape- sacrificial, unconditional "God's Love." The more we strive to become like Christ, the more we will show love to others.

God's love is unconditional and has no boundaries. In spite of all of our baggage God still loves us. Nothing can separate us from the love of God.

Romans 8: 38-39 KJV tells us, For I am persuaded, that neither death, nor life, nor angels, nor principalities, nor powers, nor things present, nor things to come, Nor height, nor depth, nor any other creature, shall be able to separate us from the love of God, which is in Christ Jesus our Lord.

Paul tells us in 1 Corinthians 13 that Love is Patient, Kind, does not envy, does not boast, it is not proud, is not rude, it is not self seeking: is not easily angered, it keeps no record of wrong. Love never fails.

God's love is action, unconditional and sacrificial. God the Father put His love into action when He sent His only son to die on the cross for you and me, so that we could have eternal life. John 3:16-17 KJV For God so loved the world that he gave His only begotten son, that whosoever believeth in him should not perish, but have everlasting life. For God sent not his son into the world to condemn the world; but that the world through him might be saved.

Suggested Songs
O How I Love Jesus
Yes Jesus Loves Me
Love Lifted Me

Reflections:

Positivity

Positive and negative thoughts or actions are choices. When we have a negative thought let us try our best to replace it with a positive thought or action.

Our actions can be negative or positive. The way we speak about something or someone, the tone of our voice as well as our body language, facial expressions represent our attitude.

Proverbs 15:1 says, A soft answer turns away wrath, but a harsh word stirs up anger. This means that if we speak kindly and softly, there is a greater possibility that an angry person will or might become calmer. When we find yourself being or becoming negative, remember this formula using the keys found on the computer keyboard

CTRL= CONTROL YOUR LANGUAGE
ALT = ALTER YOUR ATTITUDE
DEL = DELETE NEGATIVITY (HIT THAT KEY)
ENTER POSITIVITY

Start your day with a positive thought.

Suggested Song
Speak To My Heart

Reflections:

8

Inhale Courage Exhale Fear

Inhale is to breathe in, Courage is defined as the ability to do something that frightens us and motivates us to realize that we can do the task that is set before us. Do you recall Thomas the Little train that said "I think I can?" Well COURAGE gives us that umph to say confidently I KNOW I CAN!!

Exhale means to breathe you. Fear is an unpleasant emotion that causes us to believe that something or someone is dangerous. What does the spirit of fear do to us? Our spirit is the part of us that connects with God. When our spirit is clogged with fear, our connection to God is affected.

Fear will cause us to be all over the map. We will experience perspiring, knees trembling shaky hands to name a few. Fear will outright stifle and hold us back. depriving us of knowing our full potential. This is when we must remember and apply what 2 Timothy 1:7 KJV tells us, God has not given us a spirit of fear; but of POWER and of LOVE and a sound mind. If we exercise this verse we will be able to stand boldly to take on the task that is set before us.

Suggested Song
Encourage yourself

Reflections:

Grow In Christ

When a seed is placed in soil and water, the seed begins to take in water through the seed coat. As it takes up more water the seed expands and the seed coat cracks open.

The embryo inside the seed is made up of a small shoot and a small root. The root is the first to emerge from the seed. This process cannot take place in dry or oversaturated soil. It needs to be nurtured with rich soil and sunlight.

When the seed is cared for and goes through the process it becomes the beautiful plant, flower or tree that we have waited for to come forth. Like the seed we must go through a growth process. Question, How do we grow in Christ? (1) we must saturate our lives in rich soil. which is the word of God, letting it take root. Unlike the seed we can never be oversaturated with the word of God. (2) Spend time with God, listening to His voice and (3) through prayer. (talking to God).

It is then that you will begin to grow and blossom into the vessel or instrument that he wants you to be, as well as a servant that he can use.

2 Peter 3:18 KJV states, But grow in the grace and knowledge of our Lord and Savior Jesus Christ. To Him be the glory both now and forever more amen.

Suggested Song

How Great Thou Art.

Reflections:

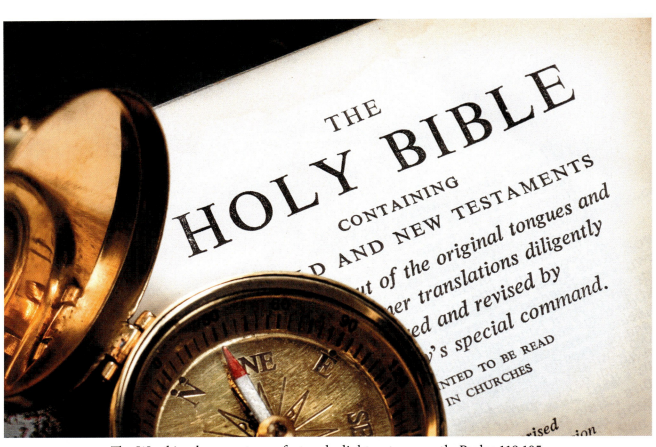

Thy Word is a lamp unto my feet and a light unto my path. Psalm 119:105.

The Bible Is Our Compass

The compass is used to determine destination. Psalm 119:105 KJV reads, Thy word is a lamp unto my feet and a light unto my path.

Have you ever prepared to go somewhere and need directions on how to get there? What did you do before the era of the GPS? (1) we got lost, (2) purchased a map and mapped out the route,(3) you had AAA or a travel agency map out the route, (4) you asked someone on the street for directions (5) you asked the gas station attendant. Today, we have the help of Google and the GPS to direct us to our destination.

So it is with the Bible, it is our compass. The GPS and maps will guide us on our path in our everyday life. The Bible is our guide and gives instructions for any situation that we will encounter. It works well in all types of weather and it won"t malfunction. We can become malfunctionable by not reading and following its instructions, Proverbs 3:6 KJV reads, In all thy ways acknowledge Him and He will direct thy path.

Let us use our compass, the Bible to guide us in the right direction so that we will arrive at our destination by doing these three things using the acronym:

F=FOLLOWING GOD'S WORD
O=OBEYING GOD'S WORD
R=READING GOD'S WORD.

Our compass is the word of God.

Suggested Songs
    Where He Leads Me
    Walk with Me
    Lord Hold My Hand

Reflections:

The Light In The Room

When you walk into a dark room, what is the first thing you do? You reach for the device that activates the light so that you can see.

Let's use a dark kitchen as an example. When the light is activated, you can see where everything is, as well as you can see if things are out of place. When you walk into a room, what do you bring? Is it love or indifference, joy or hopelessness, peace or conflict, longsuffering or impatience, gentleness or unkindness, goodness or evilness, faith or unbelief, meekness or arrogance, temperance or excessiveness?

A life filled with the light of JESUS, who is the generator of light will shine a light that is bright and will draw people to the light, not a light that will drive people away. Is the light of your presence obvious when you enter or leave the room? Let your light so shine before men that they may see your good works and glorify your Father which is in heaven. Matthew 5:16 KJV.

When we read God's word and do our best to apply His word to our life, it helps us to know what we are to bring into the room.

I encourage you to BE THE LIGHT IN THE ROOM, so that upon leaving the room someone's darkness will become brighter.

Suggested Song

This Little Light of Mine

Reflections:

God's Timing Is Not Our Timing

Many times on this journey of life we set goals. Goals that we want to attain by a certain time in our life. It's perfectly alright to plan, but while planning, we must remember that God has the masterplan for our life.

Our first plan is usually to buy a car, buy a home, finish school, take a vacation or start a family. When you set out to accomplish these goals, ask the Lord to order your steps so that you are stepping in the direction that will lead you in the direction to reach your goals according to HIS TIMING Be prayerful That your plans will line up with HIS timing and plan. When you. seek directions from the Lord you will always be in line. Psalm 37:23 NKJV, tells us The steps of a good man are ordered by the Lord and He delights in his way.

Your plan may be 1, 2, 3, 4. God's plan for you may go 1, 4, 2, 3. For you to be on His timetable. Jeremiah 29:11 KJV tells us, "For I know the plans I have for you, ''declares the Lord," plans to prosper you and not to harm you, plans to give you hope and a future.

God's timing is perfect and HIS timing cannot be timed. God has the final say I encourage you to trust God's timing, not your own. Remember God is NEVER LATE HE'S ALWAYS ON TIME.

Suggested Song

He's An On Time God

Reflections:

Surrender

When a person breaks the law and is captured, they are arrested and taken into custody. Then there is a booking process. The law enforcer records the suspect's full name and the circumstances of the alleged crime. If not captured, the person may be on the run, running from the law.

Let's take the individual that is on the run. He or she may run for a long time, hiding here and there. At some point the decision is made to surrender and turn themself in. He goes through the booking process and is detained for a certain amount of time. Eventually the person goes before the judge with his attorney and is given a sentence. Oftentimes the charges are dropped.

Before a person decides to surrender their life to Christ, they are captive and guilty of sin. When they go before the JUDGE, JESUS, He already know their full name and the circumstances of all the crimes committed, By surrendering their life to Christ, It"s because of God's grace,, God's mercy,, God's forgiveness, Jesus going to Calvary and the person's belief the charges are dropped Ephesians 2:8 KJV "For it is by grace you have been saved through faith and this is not from yourselves. It is the Gift of God."

Now you have a clean slate. CASE DISMISSED!!!!!!!

The Song writer penned the lyrics. I was guilty of all the charges, doomed and disgrace, but Jesus with His special love saved me by His grace, He pleaded and He pleaded, He pleaded my case. I'm so glad Jesus dropped the charges, Jesus and now I'm saved through grace and faith.

Suggested Songs
    Jesus Paid It All
    I Surrender All

Reflections:

The Designer's Original

You are fearfully and wonderfully made, states Psalm 139:14 KJV. The word wonderfully is the Hebrew word Pala, which means to be separated, distinguished or unique. God created you to be different or unique. The question comes to my mind, How did God make you different or unique? The answer, He made you in His image. Genesis 1:27 KJV. says, So God created man in His image, in the image of God created he him, male and female created he them. Genesis 5:1 KJV tells us This is the book of generations of Adam. In the day that God created man,in the likeness of God made he him; of all the people in the world God made ONLY ONE YOU. Don't try to be a replica of no one else. Think for a moment of the millions of dollars that are spent on people trying to recreate themselves. Even when the surgeon performs surgery on you, he or she cannot put you back together like God created you.

God likes diversity! He created you exactly how he wanted you to be. God makes no mistakes!!! Psalm 139:13 NIV reads, For you created my innermost being. You knit me together in my mother's womb. Jeremiah 1:5A KJV tells us, Before I formed thee in the belly I knew thee, let it be your prayer that God will help you to become the masterpiece that He has created you to be.

Remember, you are The Designer's Original.

Song:

God Made Me
Composer: Margaret Douroux

Reflections:

I am above all things,
I can turn around
Your situation.
- God.

Turn It Over To Jesus

You are faced with a problem and you don't know what to do. You think there's no way out. You can't see the light at the end of the tunnel and your mind is in a whirlwind trying to figure things out. You think that you're the problem solver, but you're not. Turn it over to Jesus.

We get in God's way by trying what we think will solve the problem, only to realize that everything that we have tried has failed. Look to the hills from whence cometh your help. Turn it over to Jesus in prayer and patience believing that He has the solution to the problem. Prayer changes things and prayer changes people.

What does the Bible say about casting our cares? 1 Peter 5:7 KJV states, Cast your cares on the Lord and He will sustain you; He will never let the righteous be shaken. Philippians 4:6 KJV tells us, Be careful for nothing; but in everything by prayer and supplication with thanksgiving let your request be made known unto God.

Once you have casted your cares on the Lord, don't go back and pick them up as we often do, because you think or feel that God is not moving fast enough.

Cast your cares, leave your cares with Jesus. Turn them over to Him.

Song:
Leave It There

Reflections:

Trust

Webster defines the word TRUST as the firm belief in something or someone.

What are some examples of trust? When you are in need of an attorney, you retain him or her to apply the law to help you with your situation. When you break a bone you go to an orthopedist to be casted or the bone is reset. Oh the nagging pain of a toothache, you hurry up and get in touch with your dentist to get relief as quickly as possible. Now, let me give you an everyday common example of trust. When you sit in a chair, you don't test it to see if it's sturdy enough to hold you, you just automatically sit down trusting that it will hold you. That's putting your trust in something.

When you present yourself to one of the professionals that I mentioned above you trust that the problem you are having will be corrected, solved or get better. Wouldn't it be wonderful if we could put our complete trust in the Lord as we do the professionals? especially the chair.

What does God's word say about trust? Proverbs 3:5 tells us, Trust in the Lord with all thine heart and lean not unto thine own understanding. We are to trust God at all times no matter what the situation is. We shouldn't depend on what we think we know. Trust God's lead and His guidance. He knows the road ahead.

Suggested Song
I Will Trust in The Lord

Reflections:

Boldness In Christ And Boldness For Christ

You can be bold in Christ when His word abides in you. Bold used as an adjective is defined as, showing or requiring a daring spirit.

Ephesians 6:20 KJV says, For which I am an ambassador in bonds, that therein I May speak boldly as I ought to speak.

As His word abides in you, you can be bold for Christ when you take a stand for Him according to His word.

Whenever you're asked to take on a task that is totally new to you, How do you react? Shaky hands, voice trembling, nervous stomach, some will even breakout in a sweat. All of these things are natural. What do you do with these natural characteristics? That's when we have to call upon 2 Timothy 1:7 KJV, which reads, God has not given us a spirit of fear: but of love and a sound mind. We have power that we forget we have. It is the power of the Holy Spirit that will help us to overcome the things that keep us from being bold.

When you are Bold in Christ and Bold for Christ, remember that He is always with you. You are never alone. Deuteronomy 3:8 KJV reads, The Lord himself goes before you and will be with you: he will never leave nor forsake you. Do not be afraid; do not be dismayed.

So whatever assignment God has given you, do it boldly and with confidence as unto the Lord. Acts 4:29 KJV reads, And now Lord look upon their threats and grant to your servants to continue to speak your word with all boldness. Joshua 1:9 reads, Have I not commanded you? Be strong and courageous. Do not be frightened and do not be dismayed, for the Lord your God is with you wherever you go. Whatever you do that is in His will and in His name will give you the courage to be bold.

REMEMBER, BE BOLD IN CHRIST AND BE BOLD FOR CHRIST.

Suggested Songs
Stand up Stand up
Never Alone

Reflections:

Prayer

What is prayer? Prayer is simply having a conversation with God. Did you know that reading your Bible and praying is a sure way to build a relationship with God? When we talk to God we're communicating with Him. When we read God's word He's talking to us. The posture of the body is not important, but what is important is the sincerity of the heart.

When we pray, pray knowing that God will answer according to His timing and according to His will. Mark 11:24 states, Therefore I tell you, whatever you ask in prayer, believe that you have received it and it will be yours.

Sometimes we are very impatient when we pray. When we don't get an answer when we think we should, doubt creeps in. Doubting causes us to think that God is not listening nor is he hearing us. Psalm 66:19 KJV tells us, But verily God hath heard me; he hath attended to the voice of my prayer. We want an answer right now. I suggest that you be patient and wait on the Lord.

God waits patiently for us to come to Him to make our requests known. God being the all knowing God that he is, already knows what we are in need of before we ask. Philippians 4:6 KJV states, Be careful for nothing: but in everything by prayer and supplication with thanksgiving let your request be made known unto God.

I encourage you to continue to talk with God and to pray without ceasing.

Suggested Song
Have a Little Talk With Jesus

Reflections:

The Butterfly and the Cross

The butterfly goes through four stages of development before it becomes a butterfly. That process is called metamorphosis. The four stages are: STAGE 1-EGG, STAGE 2- CATERPILLAR, STAGE 3-COCOON (CHRYSALIS), STAGE 4- ADULT (BUTTERFLY). When the process of metamorphosis is completed, the life of a beautiful butterfly emerges.

The human goes through the developmental stage by starting out as an EGG. being born into sin, to adulthood. Psalm 51:5 KJV, states, Behold, I was shapen in iniquity and in sin did my mother conceive me.

As we grow through the developmental stages, we are fed physical food that nurtures us to become healthy adults. We are also fed the word of God, which is our spiritual food that will help us to do what 2 Peter 3:18 tells us, But grow in the grace and in the knowledge of our Lord and savior Jesus Christ. To him be glory both now and forever. Amen.

Somewhere along the line in our developmental stage we are introduced to the plan of salvation:

A-Admit to being a sinner

B-Believe in His death, dying on the cross to save from sin. His Burial-buried in the grave, His Resurrection, He arose.

C-Confess what you believe. Rev. 10:9, tells us, That if thou shalt confess with thy mouth the Lord Jesus Christ and shalt believe in thine heart that God raised him from the dead thou shalt be saved. Jesus died on the cross so that you and I have eternal life John 3:16 For God so loved the world that he gave His only begotten son, that whosoever believeth in him should not perish, but have everlasting life.

When you accept the plan of salvation, you now have a new life in Christ. You can do as the butterfly, emerge out of the cocoon. You can emerge out of the cocoon of sin into a new life. You are free. Romans 6:5-7 tells us Verse (5) For if we have been planted together in the likeness of his death, we shall be also in the likeness of his resurrection: (6) knowing this, that our old man is crucified with him that the body of sin might be destroyed, that henceforth we should not serve sin. (7) For he that is dead is freed from sin.

Paul tells us in 2 Corinthians 5:17, Therefore if any man be in Christ, he is a new creature: old things are passed away; behold all things are become new.

Suggested Songs

Change Me O God

If Any Man Be In Christ

Changed

Reflections:

The Color Purple

The color purple is obtained by blending the two colors of red and blue together. In the bible, Lydia of Thyatira is known as the seller of purple. She created purple by boiling marine snails that would create the dark reddish purple hue, which was a very expensive dye. The story of Lydia can be found in the 16th chapter of Acts.

The bible mentions purple in Luke 16:19 (KJV), which reads, There was a rich man which was clothed in purple and fine linen and fared sumptuously everyday. I have read that Queen Elizabeth forbad anyone to wear purple except for those members of the Royal Family.

Purple symbolizes Royalty. What comes to your mind when you hear the word royalty? Wealth, precious stones, high priest, kings, queens, Prince and princess, tiaras crowns beautiful gowns and inheritance. These treasures here on earth will tarnish, decay and fade away. There are those that look to their family for inheritance.

Here's some good news. When you accept Jesus, the Son of God who is the King of Kings and ruler of everything, you then become the son or daughter of the TRUE ROYAL FAMILY. You will receive a crown that will not tarnish, become an heir of salvation and everlasting life. These are the benefits of being a member of the Royal Family. I Peter 2:9-10 reads But ye are a chosen generation, a royal priesthood, an holy nation, a peculiar people, that ye should shew forth the praises of him who hath called you out of darkness into his marvelous light: which in time past were not a people, but are now the people of God; which had not obtained mercy.

I encourage you to accept Jesus as your personal savior so that you can reap the benefits of being a member of the TRUE ROYAL FAMILY.

Suggested Song
   I'm a Child of The King

Reflections:

The Master Architect

Can you recall the bedtime story of The Three Little Pigs? Two of them used sticks and straw to build their house. The wolf came along and blew their house down. This lets us know that their house was not built on a sturdy foundation. The wolf was not able to destroy the third pig's house because he used bricks as a sturdier foundation.

Some of us have had the opportunity to become homeowners. The decision is made to purchase the home or build it yourself with the help of a contractor or contractors. When you decide to purchase a home you will be shown many possibilities to select from. Whether you decide to purchase or build, many factors are taken into consideration. To name a few factors in the process, seek GOD'S GUIDANCE, pricing, square footage, is the foundation sturdy? number of rooms, location, is it near a school if you have children?

When the time comes to build YOU MUST LAY THE FOUNDATION, have your blueprint that helps you with knowing how much material is needed. Make sure that the materials are of good quality. Those things are needed for man to build a house. Psalm 127:1 (KJV) reads, Except the Lord builds the house, they labor in vain that built it. It is worthless to build a house without depending on the Lord. As believers we are in the construction business of building our lives, our families and our church. (KINGDOM BUILDING)

The question comes to my mind, HOW CAN WE BUILD OUR HOUSE? (1) PRAYER: Talk to the Lord about all decisions. 1 Peter 5:7 (KJV) instructs to Cast all your cares upon Him. (2) STUDY :.Study God's word. So that we will be on the right path, because His word is a compass for our lives. Proverbs 3:6. Tell us, In all thy ways acknowledge Him and He shall direct thy path. (3) APPLICATION: Apply what you have studied in God"s word, it will help you to stand on a firm foundation. Not sinking sand.

What does the Bible say about building a house? By wisdom, a house is built and through understanding, it is established through knowledge, its rooms are filled with rare and beautiful treasures." Proverbs 24:3-4. "Therefore, if anyone who hears these words of mine and puts them into practice is like a wise man who built his house on the rock. Matthew 7:24 (KJV).

A songwriter penned these words to a song, please be patient with me, God's not through with me yet. We're always under construction and The Lord accepts us with all of our frailties and imperfections. For after all God is our MASTER ARCHITECT..

Suggested Songs
   The Solid Rock
   The Wise Man

Reflections:

The Potter and the Clay

Isaiah 64:8 KJV reads, But, now o Lord, thou art our father, we are the clay and thou our potter; and we are all the work of thy hand.

The definition of a potter is a person who shapes pots, bowls and vases out of clay. Clay is a thick heavy material from the earth, and is pliable when water is added to it, which makes it easy to shape and mold. The clay becomes hard when fired and baked in a kiln.

The potter puts a portion of clay on his wheel, as it spins he guides it with his hands to shape and mold it into a finished item. With the help of the potter's hands, the wheel helps to smooth out any imperfections and jagged edges the clay might have.

Now, let us look at the potter and the clay through a different lens. We are formed by God. God being the potter and we are the clay.. Just like the clay in the hand of the potter, we are the clay in the hand of our father, the potter. Genesis 2:7 KJV, And the Lord God formed man of the dust of the ground and breathed into his nostrils the breath of life and man became a living soul. The Bible tells us that God made us in his own image. Genesis 1:27. KJV, reads, So God created man in his own image, in the image of God created he him; male and female created he them.

Our father, the potter, is willing to repair our cracks, our brokenness and jagged edges if we are willing to trust the process of being repaired. If you are broken, he will mend you. If you are wounded he will heal you. If you are hopeless, Jesus will give you hope.. If you are empty, he will fill you. If you are guilty, you will be pardoned. He welcomes you with outstretched arms just as you are!

I just want to encourage you to allow God to break you, melt you, and mold you into the vessel that he purposed you to be.

Suggested Songs
Just As I Am
God Made Me

Reflections:

We are cleansed and covered by His blood.

The Cleanser-Sanitizer

In the year 2020, the whole world was affected by Covid 19/Corona Virus. The Virus claimed many lives and some of us lost family members and friends to this deadly disease.

Hospitals and clinics prepared to give the injection. We were encouraged to get the injection, wash our hands thoroughly, wear a mask, and allow six feet of distance between you and the next person. We were to basically sanitize anything we handled.

The sale of lysol, hand sanitizers, pine sol and hand wipes escalated to an all time high. These items could scarcely be found to purchase for a period of time and when they could be found, they were very expensively priced. While cautiously abiding by the health and safety guidelines, it was not a guarantee that you would not be affected by the virus. These guidelines were put into place to cleanse, protect and lower the possibility of transmitting the virus from one to another.

Now, let us take a look at the cleansing power of the blood of Jesus. Sometimes we have to wash a garment more than once to get rid of the stain. Jesus shed His blood ONE time on calvary for you and me to cleanse the stain of sin.1 John 1:7c KJV: and the blood of Jesus His Son cleanses us from all sin. Real cleansing from the guilt, shame and the penalty of sin came with Jesus, the lamb of God who takes away the sin of the world. Though your sins be as scarlet they shall be as white as snow. Isaiah 1:18A.KJV

The songwriter penned the words to this song, What can wash away my sins? nothing but the blood of Jesus, what can make me whole again? Nothing but the blood of Jesus. O precious is thy flow that makes me white as snow, no other fount I know, Nothing but the blood of Jesus.

Suggested Song
Nothing But The Blood

Reflections:

Christ died to set us free!!

From Slavery to Freedom

By natural birth we were born into this world of sin. **Psalm 51:5** states: Behold, I was shapen in iniquity and in sin did my mother conceive me. Because of sin we are shackled and bound by it.

The good news is, you don't have to remain in sin. You can be freed. The question comes to my mind, How can one be freed from sin? It's as simple as ABC. When you learn of Christ's death, burial and resurrection and you want to be freed, you must **A-Admit** that you are a sinner and ask for forgiveness. Romans 3:23 reads, All have sinned and fall short of the glory of God. **B-Believe**, Believe that Jesus died on the cross and rose again as payment for your sins. Romans 5:8 But God demonstrated His own love for us, in that while we were still sinners, Christ died for us. **C-Confess** and **Choose** to allow God to be in charge of your life. Romans 10:10 reads, For with the heart of man believes unto righteousness; and with the mouth confession is made unto salvation.

Our freedom from sin is made possible because Jesus died on the cross to save us from sin, so that we can have eternal life. If you have not accepted the gift of God's Son, Jesus, I want to let you know, He's waiting on you to accept the most precious gift that you could ever receive I want to encourage you to receive the gift. When you receive the gift you will be freed from the slavery of sin and move into the freedom of having an everlasting life.

Suggested Song:
   I'm Free

Reflections:

True Colors

When you see a rainbow in the sky with its beautiful array of colors, What comes to your mind? We think of God's promises which he keeps and God's faithfulness even though we are often faithless. The rainbow also reminds us of the beautiful colors of springtime. When reading Genesis 9:11-17 it informs us that God sealed his promise with a rainbow in the sky that we sometimes see after a shower of rain.

The Biblical purpose of the rainbow also represents God's protection as it is mentioned in Genesis 9:11-17. God's promise is that those who believe in Jesus and are baptized for the forgiveness of sin will be saved.

Friends and sometimes family members will make you a promise and don't keep their promise. Just remember, God is above man, true to His word and will always keep His promise. Be assured that God's promises are sure.

Now, I will tell you about some colors on the color palette: **Red** represents The blood of Jesus. 1 John 1:7 The Blood of Jesus cleanses us from all sin.. **Green** represents Growth, 2 Peter 3:18A, But Grow in grace and in the knowledge of our Lord and Savior Jesus Christ. **Black** represents Sin. Sin separates us from God. Romans 6:23, For the wages of sin is death, but the gift of God is eternal life in Christ Jesus our Lord. **White** represents Purity. Isaiah 1:18A, Though your sins be as scarlet they shall be as white as snow. **Blue** represents Baptism of repentance. Our sin nature is buried in Christ. Romans 6:4,Therefore we are buried with Him by baptism unto death, so that as Christ was raised from the dead through the glory of the Father, so we too might walk in the newness of life. **Gold** represents Heaven. Revelation 21;18-21.The material of the wall was jasper, and the city was pure gold, like clear glass. We shall live in the city of Gold. **Purple** represents Royalty, 1 Peter 2:9 But ye are a chosen people, a royal priesthood, a holy nation, God's special possession that you may declare the praises of him who called you out of the darkness. .

From now on when you see these colors on the color palette and these scriptures in the bible, prayerfully they will have a new meaning to you and help you to become aware of having a new life in Christ.

Suggested Song

God Put a Rainbow in The Sky or one of your choosing.

Reflections:

Knowing Who You Are In Christ

God's Family

When we were born into this world, we didn't get to choose our family. As we grew up we were taught our name, age, mother and father's name, the month, date and year we were born, and that we're the daughter or son of Timothy and Priscilla Williams. This was taught to us to help us establish our identity in our family.

Although God chose us, by accepting Christ as your savior, you are given the privilege of choosing you family and establishing your identity in Christ. If you are ever asked the question, who are you in Christ? You can boldly say: **I'm a CHILD OF GOD. John** 1:12 KJV, But as many as received him, to them gave he power to become the Sons of God, even to them that believe on his name. **I BELONG TO GOD.** 1 Corinthians 6:20 KJV. Ye are bought with a price; (His blood) therefore glorify God in your body, and in your spirit, which are God's. **I AM BORN AGAIN**. 1 Peter 1:23 KJV, Being born again, not of corruptible seed, but of incorruptible, by the word of God, which liveth and abideth forever. **I AM VICTORIOUS,** 1 Corinthians 15:57 KJV. But thanks be to God, which giveth us the victory through our Lord Jesus Christ. **I AM FAMILY.** Ephesians 2:19 KJV, Now therefore ye are no more strangers and foreigners, but fellow citizens with the saints, and the household of God. **I AM CHOSEN.** John 15:16 KJV, You have not chosen me, but I have chosen you, and ordained you, that ye should go and bring forth fruit, and that your fruit should remain: that whatsoever ye shall ask of the Father in my name, he may give it you.

I AM UNIQUE. Psalm 139: 14 KJV. I will praise thee; for I am fearfully and wonderfully made; marvelous are thy works; and that my soul knoweth right well. **I AM LOVED.** Jeremiah 31:3 KJV. The Lord hath appeared of old unto me; saying, yea I have loved thee with an everlasting love: therefore with lovingkindness have I drawn thee.

Now, there are benefits in knowing who you are in Christ. You can have an everlasting life, you can build a relationship with him and he will walk with you everyday. Knowing him helps you to know of his love for you. Knowing him helps you to learn to accept yourself. Knowing who you are in Christ anchors you when you are faced with circumstances of everyday life situations.

I encourage you to accept The Lord as your Savior. Know who you are in Christ and become a part of God's great big family.

Remember, YOU ARE WHO GOD SAYS YOU ARE!!!!!

Suggested Song
Draw Me Nearer

Reflections:

The Gift

Luke 2:1-7

A gift is something given voluntarily without payment in return, as to show favor toward someone or honor an occasion.

I think that we would all agree that, we all like receiving gifts at some point in our life. We exchange gifts as a sign of appreciation and gratitude, also there are countless reasons that gifts are given, exchanged or received. To name a few, it may be for an anniversary, retirement, birthday, graduation, Christmas, weddings, valentine, or a thinking of you gift. There are times you may even purchase a gift for yourself. Did you know, there are people that you come into contact with that give a gift with the expectation of receiving one in return?

The gift can come beautifully wrapped in eye catching paper and bows. They can be delivered by services such as Amazon, FedEx, the postal service or just simply delivered by hand. However the gift is delivered, we are glad and excited to be the recipient.

Now, let us look at a gift from another angle. One cold night in the city of Bethlehem, God gave us the gift of His Son Jesus voluntarily in a stable with only Joseph and the animals. Mary gave birth to the Christ Child. He was wrapped in swaddling clothes and laid in a manger filled with hay. Mind you, he was not just an ordinary baby. He is Jesus the Son of God, who was gifted to save the world.

That night the world was presented with the world's greatest gift that anyone could receive, Jesus the Son of God.

I leave you with this question, Will you open your heart today and receive the world's greatest gift? I encourage you to receive the world's greatest gift and let Him become the Lord and Savior of your life.

Song Selection:
What Shall I Render

Reflections:

The Flight /Departure

So, you've decided to take a vacation and you prefer to take to the sky. There are some things that need to be done to prepare for your flight. (1) Decide where you are going. (2) Contact a travel agent. (3) Search the airline for a reasonably priced fare. (4) Save Money (5) Secure lodging. That's how you prepare for a domestic or international flight.

Now that you have taken care of the details of your vacation and you know everything you need to know about your trip, you're excited and anticipating the day of your departure. But we can't forget how important it is to know the time of your flight's departure. If you're late you will get left behind.

Let's take a look at a spiritual flight. This time we're not contacting Samuel, the travel agent, we're making contact with Jesus, the ultimate tour guide, because He will guide you where you are to go. 1 Corinthians 11:1 KJV reads, Be ye followers of me, even as I am also of Christ. After accepting and confessing Christ as your Savior, you have made the decision as to where you want to go. Heaven becomes your new destination. The price of your ticket is free for you, because Jesus paid the price in full when He shed His blood for you and me. You don't even have to concern yourself about cancellations or rescheduling. When the Lord is ready for you to take the flight, canceling or rescheduling are not a part of the plan.

Now, about your lodging, no worries, it's also free. Jesus has many mansions and he has prepared a place for you. John 14:2-3, KJV reads, In my Father's house are many mansions: if it were not so, I would have told you. (3) And if I go and prepare a place for you, I will come again, and receive you unto myself; and where I am there ye may be also.

Remember, before we talked about the importance of knowing the day and time of your flight's departure. However, your spiritual departure is unknown, only the Father knows. Matthew 24:36 KJV reads, But of that day and hour knoweth no man, not even the angels of heaven, but my father.

I leave you with these two questions. Will you be ready for His return? Matthew 24:44 KJV reads: Be ye also ready for in such an hour as ye think not, the son of man cometh. Are you prepared to take your flight?

Suggested Songs
    I'll fly Away
    Follower of Christ

Reflections:

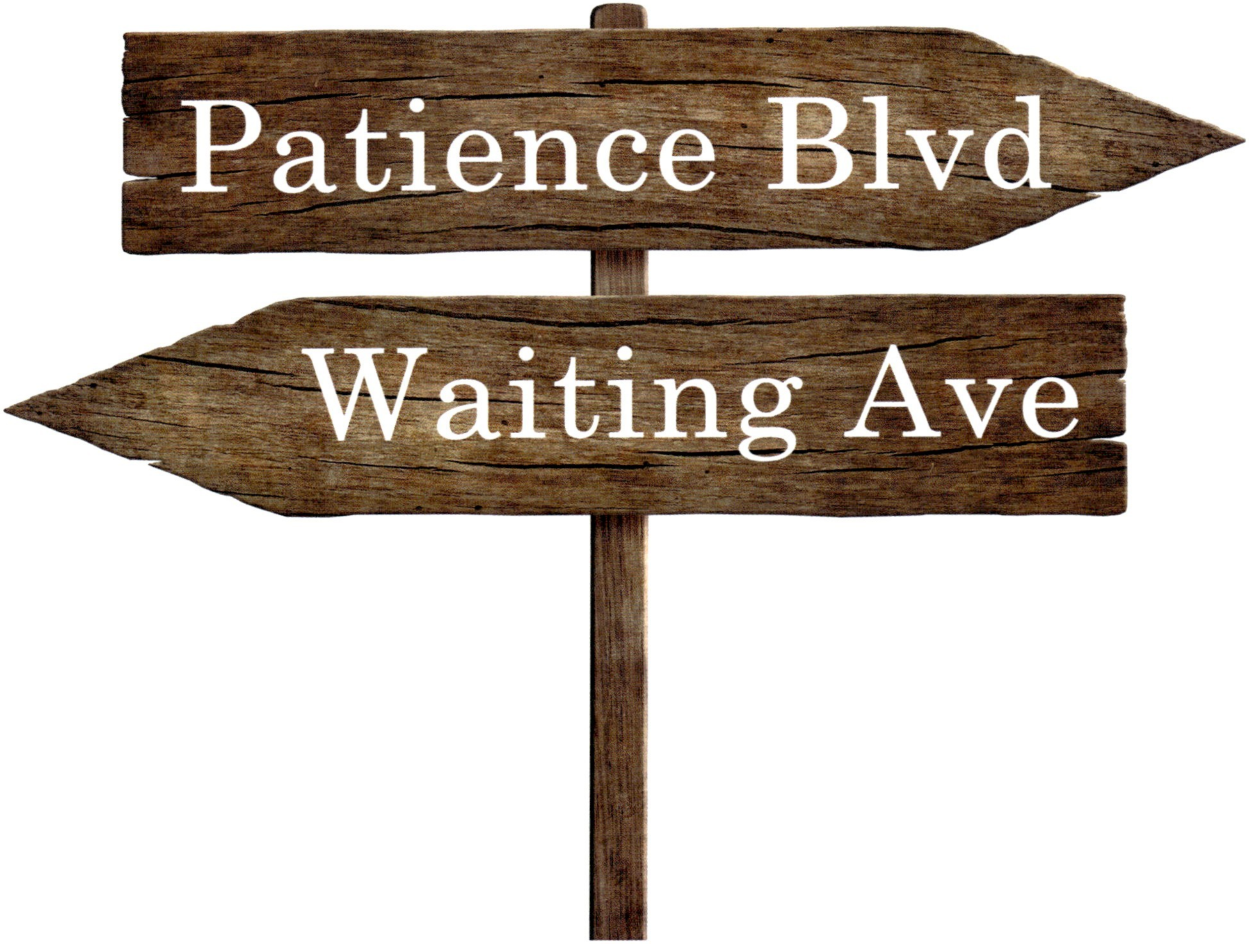
Patience Blvd
Waiting Ave

Patience-Waiting

I posed this question to a few of my friends. What is your weakest link when it comes to you having patience? These are some of the responses that were given. (1) Standing in long lines. (2) Giving a situation time to be resolved. (3) arguing. (4) My children. (5) People are not being timely. (6) Waiting on the Lord. As you read the list, other weak links probably came to your mind. Would you agree with me that we all have room for growth in the area of practicing patience.

When we are faced with situations that test our patience and waiting, a testimony can be born from that situation. Romans 8:28 KJV tells us, And we know that all things work together for good to them that love God, to them who are called according to his purpose. His purpose is for our growth. The" all things" in the above scripture include the things that try our patience.

When it comes to waiting, Psalm 37 tells us that we are to rest in the Lord, and wait patiently for Him. What does God say about patience? Do not be anxious about anything, but in prayer and pleading with thanksgiving let your request be made known to God. Philippians 4:6 NASB.

Let's Keep in mind, Patience requires waiting and waiting requires patience.

Suggested Song:
Please Be Patient With Me

Reflections:

Apply Now!

Availability and Ability

You have been out of a job for weeks, those weeks have now turned into months. Your quest has become finding employment. Right now your new job is looking for a job.

A friend informs you that a certain toy store is hiring. Knowing that you have the ability and you are available, you apply for the position. Now you are anxiously and patiently waiting to hear from the company. To your dismay you received the call that you've been waiting for, only to be told that you didn't get the position because you didn't meet the requirements and qualifications.

Let us look at employment and unemployment from a different angle. When you accept and confess Christ as your savior, you then become one of His employees. Your duties are to **spread His Word**. Mark 16:15, KJV tells us, And he said unto them Go ye into all the world and preach the gospel to every creature. **Worship him**, John 4:24 KJV tells us, God is a spirit: and they that worship him must worship him in spirit and in truth. **Love one another**. John 13:34 reads: A commandment I give unto you, That ye love one another; as I have loved you, that ye also love one another. It is also our duty to exalt Him.

The thought may come to you, that you're not qualified to carry out these duties, but remember God equips the called. Hebrew 13:20-21 reads: Now the God of peace, that brought again from the dead our Lord Jesus, that great Shepherd of the sheep, through the blood of the everlasting covenant, make you perfect in every good work to do his will working in you that which is well pleasing in his sight through Jesus Christ; to whom be glory for ever and ever. Amen.

Availability is what God wants from us rather than ability. When you avail yourself to him as Annanias, Jacob, Samuel, Moses and Abraham did you too can say, Here Am I. God Will equip you with the skills that you need to fulfill the assignment that he has for you. How will God do this? He will do it through His Word, His Spirit and His people. So read His word, listen to and obey the Holy Spirit and you will have Lifetime employment.

Suggested Song
Available To You
It Pays to Serve Jesus

Reflections:

HIDE N SEEK

Let's take a stroll back down memory lane. Can you recall as a child playing the game, Hide N Seek with your friends? One person would stand by a tree or some other designated structure. which was called homebase. That person was the seeker. He or she would cover their eyes and count to ten as the others would run to find a hiding place. they were the hiders. The seeker would open his or eyes and chant, ready or not here I come.

As the seeker tries to find the hiders, the hiders would try to make it to home base without being found or tagged by the seeker. The first one found became the next seeker and the last one found was the winner. When you seek and find God you are a winner.

Now about Hiding. We say and do things that we can hide from man, but just know that nothing is or can be hidden from God. He is all seeing and all knowing. Hebrews 4:13 NIV reads: Nothing in all creation is hidden from God's sight. Everything is uncovered and laid bare before the eyes of him to whom we must give account.

As we go through this journey of life, we are taught God's word, hear God's word and read God's word. At some point we learn that God is homebase. How do we get to God, the homebase? Jeremiah 29:13 KJV reads, And ye shall seek me and find me when ye shall search for me with your whole truth.

Unlike the rules of the game hide n seek where the seeker is finding the hiders, God is waiting for the seekers to find him. Isaiah 55:6 says: Seek ye the Lord while he may be found; call on him while he is near.

Remember when you seek and find God, YOU are a winner !!

Suggested Song:
He Hideth My Soul

Reflections:

Gifts and Talents

A gift comes effortlessly, whereas a talent is a skill that is developed by training. All are given a talent or a gift, either one can be a hobby or career. Some individuals are given the ability to sew, decorate, play an instrument, teach, sing, be a listener, or an encourager to name a few. Romans 12:4 KJV says, For just as we have many members in one body and all the members do not have the same function. We all have a designated purpose.

Whether it be a gift or talent, they both are given to us by our creator God. Every good and perfect gift is from God. James 1:17a. By working together (unity) we can function at our best if everyone uses their talent or gift in its unique role.

Whatever talent or gift that you have been blessed with, use it to edify the body of Christ. Ephesians 4:12 KJV tells us, For the perfecting of the saints, for the work of the ministry, for the edifying of the body of Christ.

Suggested Song
    Use Me Lord

Reflections:

Come As You Are

As a child growing up I had clothes that I wore to school, clothes that I played in and clothes that I wore to church, which were referred to as church or Sunday clothes. My school and play clothes were interchangeable, but my Sunday clothes were just that, they were worn on Sundays only.

Have you ever had a conversation with someone about appropriate clothing for church? If so, I'm sure that you've heard the response "God said, come as you are" Yes God wants you to come to him as you are. I believe that statement means, whatever spiritual, mental or physical condition you're in, go to him. If you're sick he will heal you. Jeremiah 17:14 KJV reads, Heal me o Lord, and I shall be healed; save me and I shall be saved; for thou art my praise. If you're lost he will save you, Romans 10:9 KJV reads.

That if thou shalt confess with thy mouth the Lord Jesus and shalt believe in thine heart that God raised him from the dead thou shalt be saved. If you're broken, he will mend you. Psalm 147:3 KJV, He healeth the broken in heart, and bindeth up their wounds. If you are guilty, he will pardon you. 1 John 1:9 KJV reads, If we confess our sins, he is faithful and just to forgive us our sins, and cleanse us from all unrighteousness.

Does Jesus love and accept us the way we are? Yes he does. God wants us to come to him with all of our imperfections and flaws. Give them to him so that he can help us change and grow to become more like Him.

So, remember when you hear the statement or comment Come as you are, it is not referring to your outer appearance, God is concerned about your inner man and your salvation.

Suggested Song
    Just As I Am

Reflections:

References

Bible Gateway
www.biblegateway.com

The Holy Bible Authorized King James Version
KJV Giant Print Reference Bible
Copyright 1998
All Rights Reserved
Holman Bible Publisher-Nashville, Tennessee

Giant Print Concordance
Copyright 1998
All Rights Reserved

Printed in the United States
by Baker & Taylor Publisher Services